How to Source Products on Amazon FBA:

A Beginners Guide to Sourcing Products to Private Label and Sell on Amazon.

Table of Contents

Introduction

If you're reading this that likely means you've heard of "selling on Amazon', "Amazon FBA" or "private label products" being bandied around online or from other entrepreneurs. Perhaps you're already quite experienced in this field and are interested in how others run their business or perhaps you're simply curious about what the fuss is all about. In a nut shell, Amazon FBA can be compared to what eBay was 10 years ago, in terms of the opportunity it provides to earn money online. The actual technicalities of how FBA and private labelling works will be covered in the next two chapters. For those that are merely curious about it, we'd guess it's because you've heard that it's a lucrative way for almost anyone to make money or a living from. Shit, maybe you've even heard that people are able to run their private label businesses from the beach and only spend an hour a day maintaining it. Despite a beautiful picture of working on the beach in leisure with your laptop by your side, sun shining overhead, and the calls of nature in the background as waves crash on the shore with birds soaring through the blue skies, trust us when we say it really isn't as fun or nice as it sounds.

There's sand everywhere! Getting into your laptop, pants, bags, and if it's a windy day, it's just blowing sand on you and the friction can be so hard the sand actually stings you. The glare from the sun on the laptop makes it insanely hard to see what's happening, especially if you've got sunglasses on. The amount of shit you have to deal with while trying to work on the beach goes on and on but if there's only one takeaway from this book, save yourself the hassle and don't try to work on the beach for anything. Okay, rant over.

It's possible you've heard claims of people making $1,000 dollars a day and this could range from groups of housewives to the unemployed making bank in a ridiculously short amount of time.

Some go even further to claim they've made millions in just their first year, and what do they do now that they're millionaires? They sell books, courses, and products about how they made they're millions. Not to rag on these people too much as we know some who are actually legit and know what they're talking about and doing, but a lot of these people out there going about touting their courses aren't offering a whole lot of value for what they're charging or are simply sharing outdated information as they aren't actively selling in the Amazon marketplace anymore as they now make their living from selling their education based products.

Needless to say, there is a viable and accessible business model in the world of Amazon's private label market with plenty of money to be made. Recently in 2016 we've heard a lot of talk of people questioning whether the Amazon marketplace is becoming too saturated with a lot more competitors these days or that Amazon is making it more difficult for new comers to establish themselves. We think all of that is a load of horseshit and are simply people trying to justify why they're failing at this business or trying to keep people out of this space for their own selfish reasons (i.e. profit). There are SO many opportunities in the marketplace with thousands of products out there that are yet to be discovered and sold by private labelers. Amazon is continuously growing and capturing more of the marketplace each day and this only results in an increase in the level of supply (customers) that will therefore increase demand (need or want of products). Amazon represented 56.9% of total e-Commerce sales in 2015 (data compiled by eMarketer) and this is only forecasted to grow here on out. Amazon is highly focused on (1) making sure customers are happy, because they know happy customers won't leave and that they will also bring even more customers to them due to the power of word of mouth and (2) making money. If you don't believe us simply watch any interview of Jeff Bezos (the CEO of Amazon) or Google what Amazon's mission statement and purpose is.

It could be argued that Amazon has made it slightly more difficult for newcomers to establish themselves with recent changes it has made to FBA, reviews, and product listing, however we see that as a positive note, not because we are already established on the marketplace but because if we were starting out, we'd know this simple fact means there will be less competition over the long term as people view this first stumbling block or obstacle and don't even start. Or if it simply delays their start, they would have wished they started sooner. We know the most pressing question you have on your mind right now, so let's talk shop and get to it.

Conservative profit estimates for your first product will lie in the range of $1,000 to $2,000 dollars a month as long as you put the work in and follow the process detailed here. This isn't to mean that in one month you will be making this amount! BUT once your product has been made, shipped, and gone through the initial marketing and launch phase, it has the potential to be making this amount, AFTER the initial legwork has been done. Depending on how much time you can dedicate and how well the stars align for you (more on this later), this initial legwork could take anywhere from 2.5 to 6 months to get going. It generally takes 3-4 months though and this isn't to say you are working full-time for these 3-4 months either. This period will mainly consist of doing research on

Amazon, going back and forth with manufacturers, and then 'patiently' waiting to get your product manufactured and shipped.

A more realistic and average expectation for a product would be about $3,000 profit a month if you've done your research thoroughly, selected a good product and followed through on the instructions closely during the initial legwork phase. The profit per month for your products would of course depend on outside factors though, such as how much capital you have available to start with and how much time you are able to dedicate to this venture. If you start out with a smaller amount of capital, your profits will be less but there's nothing wrong with that, taking fewer risks and building up slowly can be smart depending on how you work and you always have the capacity to build from there.

If you start out highly aggressive, put up a large chunk of capital early ($10,000+), and spend a ton of time hustling and grinding in the initial legwork phase, you could potentially be earning near $10,000 a month from a product after the initial marketing and launch phase. This would be a rare exception though and would apply more to people who already have experience in businesses or selling (although isn't always necessarily the case). The downside of this balls out approach of course is that you have to have time available to dedicate to this venture, and if you select the wrong product, you're capital will be tied up as you 'patiently' wait for the rest of the stock to get sold off (if it even gets sold off!) You'll learn a lot for sure if your first product is a dud, but why go through all of that when it isn't necessary.

You might have a few questions running through your head right about now. Questions like "Well, how much time will I actually need to dedicate to this then?" "How much capital or money will I need to put up for this?" Our response is for you to first of all relax, chill, and take things one step at a time. We'll cover all of this throughout the remainder of the book; we're just getting the big stuff out of the way - "How much money can I really make from this?"

This book has been designed to provide a roadmap for you to follow step by step (for the most part) to selecting the best niche or product for you so that you can create a successful private label business. It would be a lie to say everything in the business is going to be easy. The actual processes and steps we provide are easy no doubt, and you may experience slight hiccups here and there. For the most part you will just need to put in the time and effort to follow through on what's laid out for you (this is the difficult or easy part depending on you). Note that there will be struggles along the way to your success in this business. Anything worth having doesn't always come easy. We will provide the structure and roadmap for you to follow but it's up to you to TAKE ACTION and FOLLOW it through till the end. If you slack off at any point of the roadmap you will only decrease your chances of success. We're here to make sure you maximize your possibility of success.

With Amazon's Fulfillment by Amazon (FBA) option (which we like to call Freedom by Amazon) you're allowed to use the resources that Amazon has at its disposal: list a product on their marketplace website, store your products in their warehouse. Promote your products on their webstore through their marketing efforts, ship out your products and package it cheaply to customers. And most of all, they'll deal with angry customers for you.

All you're required to do is send them (or get your manufacturers to) your products packaged and labelled correctly. We like to think of FBA as Freedom by Amazon because they take care of a lot of the dirty work for us, allowing us to spend our time on more of the important things. Amazon has provided many people the opportunity to escape the rat race, build their own businesses, become their own boss and achieve financial independence and freedom. The private label business model is as close to a passive income business as possible due to minimal maintenance required once everything is set in place correctly. Ah, what a true blessing. Thank you, Jeff Bezos. Even if you are a crazy, narcissistic bastard (based on accounts of ex-Amazon employees). Mr. Bezos has even received praise from the investing magnate Warren Buffet for his business savviness and ability to please customers, not a feat to be taken lightly.

The key thing to note as we move forward from here is that picking the right products, the products that will make you money, is the crux of this business (and of course customer satisfaction but that is a byproduct of having the right product!) Once the product has been selected, and a suitable manufacturer has been found, the products can then be private labelled. Private labelling is essentially when someone else (a manufacturer) makes a product and you sell it by getting them to slap on your own private label or brand to the product. That doesn't mean you are re-labeling a can of Sprite as 'Sarah's lemonade', you would instead be buying a generic product such as a toothbrush and getting the manufacturers to physically add your private label or brand onto the toothbrushes during the production process. So you would then be selling the toothbrushes as 'Forever Clean' toothbrushes (or whatever catchy brand name you can think of). In this case perhaps at the bottom of the handle of the toothbrush a logo/brand is etched into the toothbrush with 'Forever Clean' printed above it.

Thanks to the opportunities of the internet and FBA, this business of selling isn't just available to business tycoons but for anyone with a bit of change to invest and a drive to put in the work. The process from start to end is involved and there are many factors to take into account, which is where this series of books is intended to come to the rescue. We'll start by discussing FBA and private label selling in greater detail, and then we will concern ourselves with the important step of how to pick and research the best product/niche to sell for you.

Get a notepad and paper, or whatever else you'd like to use to take notes and we'll get moving.

What is Amazon FBA Sourcing?

If you're unsure what Fulfillment by Amazon (FBA) is, yet you regularly purchase products from Amazon's marketplace, then it's most likely you have bought from sellers using FBA. When a product is listed as Fulfilled by Amazon (you can tell by looking for a note that is found above the pricing on the product page - "Sold by [Insert seller name here] and Fulfilled by Amazon") this means a third party (a party separate from Amazon and the customer) has sent the product to Amazon's warehouse where Amazon then takes over the handling and shipping of the product so it gets to the customer. In this case, we as Amazon sellers, are those third parties who supply the product to Amazon so customers can then buy it.

As discussed in the previous chapter, a seller using FBA means they don't need to rent out a warehouse to store their products and there's no added hassle of having to send out packages, deal with returns, or customer service issues. Could you imagine making daily runs to the post office to send out your products? Having to buy your own shipping supplies with packages and labels, printing them off and sticking them on to each order? Not to mention dealing with customers who want to return your products for whatever reason and angry customers calling you up to complain about a minor issue.

So, the question of course is what's the catch? Why isn't every seller in the world using this service and selling on Amazon if they're taking care of so much of the dirty work? Well, the service isn't free and Amazon doesn't allow you to send them garbage bags full of trinkets and junk in the hopes that something will sell. Amazon charges on two levels with FBA.

Once you've signed up for an Amazon seller account and begin using FBA, you will have the choice of being an individual seller or a professional seller. If you are looking to make money long term with private label products, the individual option is not feasible and is more of an option for hobbyists. An individual account is free and the only case where you would use it is if you were selling less than 40 units per month, this is because on an individual account you are charged $1 for each item you sell on Amazon not including Amazon's other fees. When you upgrade to a professional account, you get charged a monthly fee of $40 but the $1 per item sold fee is waived, so this means the breakeven point between an individual seller or professional account is selling 40 units per month. Why would you pay more than $39.99 for an individual account considering you are selling more than 40 units per month when you can upgrade to a professional account and not get charged extra fees?

Other differences between regular and professional accounts are that you won't be able to run Amazon ads without a professional account. A professional account also provides you the ability to access certain features that aren't possible with individual accounts such as Amazon Marketplace Web Services for feeds, reports, and API functions. Having a professional seller account enables greater functionality with JungleScout, a web browser extension that helps speed up research times (more on this later). You will be able to switch back and forth between an individual and professional account easily but doing this doesn't make sense if you're trying to build a profitable private label business.

The second cost from FBA comes from the services provided by Amazon for shipping and handling the product itself. You will have to pay a basic storage fee whenever a product is kept at an Amazon warehouse: the bigger or heavier the item is, the more it will cost to store and the greater the shipping costs will be. If you use their warehouses in the months leading up to the Christmas period it costs a little bit more (this is a very small cost compared to the massive increase in sales during this time), and there are additional costs to Amazon for shipping the item to the customer with other small fees and cuts Amazon takes along the way. Keep in mind, these costs are very reasonable as Amazon operates on such a large scale that they are able to provide these services at very low rates. Although these fees will eat into your overall profit margins for products, it's a part of the business and despite these fees, there are many lucrative opportunities for healthy profits to be made.

These are the costs paid directly to Amazon; FBA may incur slightly different costs that you wouldn't normally have to deal with if things are done right. Amazon has stringent rules about how products are to be received at their warehouse with correct labels and packaging to be used unless you send your products in to Amazon, so they do the packaging and labeling for you at a costly fee.

The benefits of selling on Amazon through FBA far outweigh the costs. By selling on Amazon you have the advantage of leveraging Amazon's reputation, system, and customer base of millions that visit Amazon to do their shopping. Even if products may not be the cheapest ones available online (due to Amazon's trustworthiness, reliability, and customer service) people will buy from them for the sake of convenience. No matter how much money you can theoretically make by selling directly to customers from your own website you are almost always going to sell more via Amazon and this has been our experience to date. If you are able to build a real brand name however, that is when you can consider competing with Amazon for sales on your own websites. The sales difference between the same products on Amazon and your own website can be compared to selling in a small grocery store versus having shelf space in Walmart. This is especially the case for private labelers starting out and who are just starting to build their brands.

The other advantage gained through private labeling is that we are able to build a new brand for our product. If you go out and try to sell your first product on your own website, say www.kitchengoodsdirect.com you face a lot more hurdles and obstacles. (1) No one has ever heard of you, (2) people will be a lot more hesitant to buy from you, and (3) you will have to drive traffic/customers to your site AND actually convert the traffic to buy on your website. Amazon solves all of these issues as they are associated with quality, trustworthiness, and have a ton of traffic that are already looking to convert (buy stuff) with their credit cards details on file! Amazon's customers at any one time are only a few mere clicks away from buying something.

These are the pros of selling on Amazon, and there are always cons that go with it so what are they? The first major con is that your product is being sold on Amazon's marketplace. They have total control over whether or not they will sell your product or market it to begin with. It's possible they may believe you are doing things that are violating the terms and conditions for selling on Amazon and suspend or terminate your account. You don't have full control over your business and rely heavily upon Amazon; essentially they are your boss to a degree, alongside your customers but if you don't piss off your boss or your customers you're on the safe side. The second con of course are the fees associated to selling on Amazon. However we believe this is nothing to fret over as the expenses needed to build up the processes and systems they have in place such as storing your products in a warehouse, shipping it, and dealing with customer service would be close to if not more than what is being paid.

So what's the game plan we suggest you do and consider once you're business is well established on Amazon's marketplace? Expand and diversify! First leverage Amazon's reputation and clientele and then work towards building your own brand, customer base, website, and build your own email list so you will have another option available for you to sell your products. This strategy will be discussed in greater detail in book four of the series.

FBA saves you essential time as you won't have to store and ship products, it's key to note that the real money is made from finding, sourcing, and selling the right products, you don't get paid for time spent putting labels on boxes.

One simple factor to consider with private label (and anything in life) is how you spend your time. Even if you had the room to store 1,000 dehumidifiers in your garage, how long will it take you to print the label? Package each item? Handle the shipping for orders of your product? Take into mind, you won't be selling the products in one big order and they will instead be sold in batches so that will be multiple runs weekly to ship the products out. Let's say it takes you 5 minutes for one dehumidifier that is roughly 83 hours of your time; that is one long working week that Amazon can take care of for you, leaving you more time to get on with the important tasks or things more important to you in life. With FBA, you have the amazing opportunity to sell products on one of the biggest international marketplaces in the world from the comfort of your own home.

Sourcing from local suppliers

There are a lot of ways to find products to buy and sell online. I will give you 5 of the best ways to do it.

1 - THRIFT STORES

So how do we find thrift stores that can be reseller friendly?

-

Here are some ideas to do it:

-

A- Drive Around

-

Thrift stores are everywhere! It's almost impossible not to find one specially if you're living on a pretty large city. Even small towns have a lot of them.

-

Make this activity a fun one, go on a 1-hour road trip with your kids. Tell them you're looking for stuff to buy and if they come with you, you may even give them a gift (from thrift store).

-

B - Google

If you search for thrift store + your city (or town, zipcode), you're going to find a list of stores ready for the taking.

-

See my example below.

-

"Thrift Store Baton Rouge"

thrift store baton rouge

Web   Maps   Images   Videos   More ▾   Search tools

About 73,000 results (0.44 seconds)

America's Thrift Stores - Thrift Stores - Baton Rouge, LA ...
www.yelp.com › Shopping › Thrift Stores ▾
★★★★★ Rating: 3 - 7 reviews
7 Reviews of America's Thrift Stores "Clean. Uncluttered. Discounts upon discounts.
Nice finds. Friendly staff. Ample parking. All sales ARE NOT final. Looking ...

America's Thrift Stores
www.americasthrift.com
4.2 ★★★★★ 7 Google reviews · Google+ page

(A) Mall Properties Inc. 9526
Cortana Pl
Baton Rouge, LA, United
States
+1 225-923-0010

Here Today Gone Tomorrow Thrift St...
plus.google.com
Google+ page

(B) 10240 Burbank Dr
Baton Rouge, LA, United
States
+1 225-769-2259

Goodwill
www.goodwill.org
3 Google reviews

(C) 3121 College Dr # D
Baton Rouge, LA, United
States
+1 225-926-1868

Map results for thrift store baton rouge

Baton Rouge - TheThriftShopper.com
www.thethriftshopper.com/city/Baton_Rouge/LA/1.htm ▾
Find thrift stores, charity resale vintage and consignment shops in Baton Rouge,
Louisiana Page 1.

Thrift Shops in Baton Rouge LA - Yellow Pages
www.yellowpages.com › Baton Rouge, LA ▾
Results 1 - 30 of 59 - Find 59 listings related to Thrift Shops in Baton Rouge on
YP.com. See reviews, photos, directions, phone numbers and more for the best ...

Store/Distribution Center - Society of St. Vincent de Paul ...
www.svdpbr.org/**stores**.aspx ▾
Thrift Store In 1963, the Society opened the first St. Vincent de Paul Store/Distribution
Center to assist the poor of our community In Baton Rouge we now have ...

America's Thrift Stores - New & Used Clothes, Shoes ...
www.americasthrift.com/ ▾
THRIFTY TREASURES We have something for everyone. Take a look at some of the
treasures that have been found in our stores recently View Now

Visit Our Thrift Store - Connections for Life | Baton Rouge
www.connectionsforlife.net/**thrift-store-baton-rouge**/ ▾
The Connections for Life **thrift** store assists with much-needed funding for the program.
We serve Baton Rouge and the surrounding community by providing ...

Connections for Life - Helping Women and Children Rebuild ...
www.connectionsforlife.net/ ▾
Find great bargains for a great cause at our thrift store. Every purchase you make helps
to ... Baton Rouge, Louisiana 70802 M-F 8am-6pm, Sat 8am-5pm

Baton Rouge Thrift Stores in Baton Rouge LA Yellow Pages ...
www.superpages.com › Baton Rouge, LA ▾
Results 1 - 25 of 50 - Directory of Baton Rouge Thrift Stores in LA yellow pages. Find
Thrift Stores in Baton Rouge maps with reviews, websites, phone numbers. ...

-

There are hundreds of stores like this. You don't have to be
bound by your area. A few hours of drive from a city near you is
gonna be worth it specially if you can find collectibles.

C- Maps

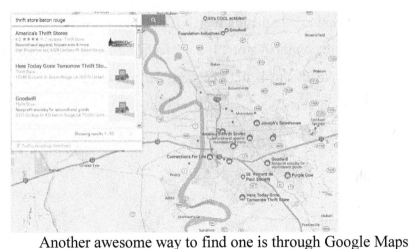

Another awesome way to find one is through Google Maps

When you search for that keyword, in my case Thrift store baton rouge, a map's going to show up where thrift store are pinned.

Click the map and navigate to an area near you.

You can use zip code to narrow your search even more. I usually get started with the stores near me since it's accessible and take very little time to find.

Some stores will be larger and much expensive than others, it all depends on your current budget and the types of product that you want to look for.

My #1 TOOL a.k.a Super Sneaky Simple Tactic

I'll reveal to you the number 1 TOOL that I always bring before I go to any thrift store. It's gonna be a life saver and you're going to make a lot of better decisions because of it.

The good news is you already have it.

- huh?

- Then what is it??....

- Your Smartphone.

- More specifically, a smartphone with internet access.

When you are looking at items, you're gonna find some items that you have no idea on whatever the heck is the value of that thing. if you have your smartphone, you can easily search for ebay, craigslist or amazon on what is the current price of that product in the market. If someone is buying an item for $200 then you know that you'll make a profit even if it cost you $100. If you didn't have your smartphone, you could have left a good $50 -$80 profit for that item.

If there's one tool I can't live without when it comes to reselling items from TS, it's gonna be my Iphone. It helps me to make better and faster decisions. I don't have to think twice if I'm gonna buy a certain item. If I know the market value of that price, I'll buy that item in a heartbeat knowing that I'm gonna make a healthy profit from it.

Technology is taking over the way we do business, use it in your advantage. Not many people are doing this simple tactic even though it's as simple as doing an Ebay search. Imagine how much money you'll be able to save from bad decisions just because you don't know the value of a certain item.

Use this, I've been hammering this for the past few sentences. But it's that important. If you don't have a smartphone, you don't have to get an Iphone, a cheap one would do as long as you can use Amazon and Ebay.

2 - Walmart

The next place to find products is Wal-Mart.

Also, you can sign up on DUBLI to get cash back for your purchases. You'll save a lot over time by using DUBLI.

Callimont Park 3-Seat Daybed Swing, Red

☆ ☆ ☆ ☆ ☆ 0 review   Q&A   Walmart # 553199169

$178⁰⁰

⊕

Quantity: 1

📦 **Shipping**
Not available ▾

This item is not ava
Walmarts within 5(

You searched:
10001

I usually find products over $50 so I can get free shipping.

This product cost $178 on WalMart

Let's check it out on Ebay.

Red 3-Seat Swing Daybed Recliner Folding Seater Shade Outdoo

Item condition: New
Ended: Feb 08 2015 11:34PM
Quantity: 1   0 available / 2 sold

Price: US $239.99

Shipping: May not ship to United Kingdom - Read item description or contact selle
for shipping options. | See details
Item location: New York, New York, United States
Ships to: United States

Delivery: Varies
Payments: PayPal VISA
Credit Cards processed by PayPal
See details

Returns: 30 days money back, buyer pays return shipping | See details
Guarantee: ebay MONEY BACK GUARANTEE | See details

After considering the fees, payments etc.

The seller will make at least $25 on every item that he will be able to sell.

If you can sell 2 of this item per week then that's a profit of $50.

Now, that doesn't seem a lot of money. That's only $200 per month. But what if you can find more of these products? Find 4 more and that's a total profit of $1,000/month!

5 x 200 = 1,000

You can then expand all you want and make a small fortune by just repeating the process.

Let us look at another product.

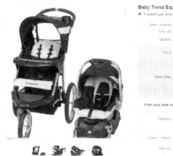

Let's go to EBAY

This one sells for $223

223 – 199 = $24

Less fees … then your profit may end up as $10 or so.

You can find hundreds of products on WalMart and sell them for a profit. If you look hard enough, you can even discover products that can give you up to $100 per item.

Other websites you can look up are:

Sears

Overstock

CHINA TOWN

Most cities today have a local China Town where you could find all kinds of products sold by Chinese people. These products are cheap and can be resold at a higher price online. Also, you don't have to worry about shipping and broken product problems because you're going to see the product firsthand.

My suggestion to you is that you spend a few hours per week looking at products to buy on ChinaTown. This could be your personal gold mine!

Sourcing from Alibaba

Product research is already discussed in volume 1 of this book. Once you get in business, you should always know who you are dealing with. My special attention was in regards to Amazon, which covered the main points, as that's going to be the main platform where you will be selling goods. It is equally important to know who you are sourcing from.

Background of Chinese culture

You might not be interested in this topic. Nonetheless, you should have a basic understanding of the cultural differences and values of the Chinese when it comes to Business.

In case you have lived there, or already done your research, you may choose to skip this part, however you might equally pick up something that could help you to build an even better Business relationship with a Chinese supplier.

In Europe as well as in the US, once business partners meet it's often a ritual that both parties like to get down straight to Business, and personally I don't hold that against anyone.

On the other hand, when going into Business with a Chinese factory, especially when both parties are from Chinese background, what you see is that in order to consider one another to be a good future Business partner they both would like to know more about each other.

It is often seen that having a meal first and talking about family, and what has been achieved previously is more important to discuss at first in order to be more comfortable with each other and being able to take the Business to the next level.

It's actually very simple to understand, once you think about it. It's always more comfortable to do Business with someone who you know. That's why in order to get the best result with a supplier you really should get into a personal contact.

Some people can't afford this. They simply just want to source product as quickly as possible without even visiting China, and that's fine too.

If you choose to meet someone in person, best practice is always to get an appointment with the Factory owner, as most times when you start making your first contact, in e-mail or a phone call, there is a possibility that you will reach the sales person at first.

Problems might occur, such as the actual Factory owner doesn't speak good English, or too busy to get an early appointment, so the second best tactic would be a Skype call, or a telephone call.

Regards to a telephone call, or Skype call, I would leave it for last, or at least for a later date, as you might not feel comfortable speaking with someone whose accent is hardly understandable.

We don't want any of this to happen. However, if you are planning to visit China, or just happen to be there in the near future, these are the best practices.

In addition, there are many trading shows, EXPO-s around the word, well known as CANTON FAIR-s, where you can have an opportunity to meet with Chinese suppliers, Factory owners, and might even find a product that is still in the development stage. You can take advantage of the fact that these products are not already listed on Alibaba, so you could become one of the first people who could potentially resell them.

I have never visited any Canton Fair, and I would personally only recommend people who are already successful in this area and know how to deal with Factory owners from previous experience.

This book will focus on how to source from China without meeting anyone, visiting Canton Fairs, or factories. However, it is only fair to introduce other methods for the reader's awareness.

GUANXI

Do not worry about having to learn Chinese, but there is something that you have to get from this:

Guanxi is translated as "networks" or "relationships", also "connections," and has another meaning when talking in Business. That is something that is crucial to have. In business context it's a must have in order to be successful. In order to secure the successful business deal, you have to understand that Chinese people always use Guanxi.

It carries elements of trust, time, and respect for each other that

has to be mutually invested. If you want to build Guanxi, having a meal, or even having a drink together can help to do so.

This means a long-term relationship off course. This is one of the main points you have to understand: factories want you to continuously do business.

Building Guanxi will not only help you have a better trust, it will get you better deals when it comes to negotiations, as well as faster responses to your enquiries. If you are able to build a strong Guanxi with your supplier, they will never try to rip you off and they will always make sure that you get the best they can provide.

Some people can build Guanxi so deep that suppliers even agree to only supply you with certain products due to reaching a high level of trust and time invested into a Business relationship.

Ethics and Values

What you need to understand is that the Chinese mentality is completely different, and you should never assume anything.

When it comes to a problem, it's in a Chinese nature not to mention anything about it, though they are aware of the problem.

Why is that? - You might ask!

With a close look at Chinese history you will realize that someone who complains about anything, for instance, something that might have been a faulty product, those are the ones that always like to make trouble – simple troublemakers. In the past those who were troublemakers were punished. So do not assume anything, especially when it comes to Quality Control.

Chinese culture relies on stability and harmony, so when someone talks about an issue, he or she is actually considered a bad person.

That is one of the main reason you might have heard wrong impression that China made products are not good quality. However, when you really think about it, it might have been an assumption of a US Entrepreneur, who had just assumed that the product will be as he or she imagined.

In reality if anything happens, it will come back to you. You as an entrepreneur have the responsibility to ask questions and be very explicit when explaining anything you want to get done.

Another assumption people face is that in Chinese culture there is nothing wrong with copying someone else's product or logo. When you visit Alibaba, you will find that hundreds of suppliers seem to have the same product. What you actually see is that in China everyone photo shops other people's products and logos.

So, do not assume anything. Be very specific that this is your logo, this is your design, and you do not want this to be published anywhere else. This is a hint. If you don't mention any of this, you might get surprised and very angry; however, in China it's completely normal.

It is always your responsibility to communicate and be very clear on your vision from the beginning. You must always keep your suppliers in touch by being proactive. The main reason is to avoid delivery of faulty products.

Your best bet is to put it in writing, and that's also why it is always better to write e-mails, using bullet points and numbers, rather than just mention it.

That's why it is very important that when you introduce yourself you must make an impression that you have a potential goal, and start building Guanxi, and if possible do it with the Factory owner.

Yes, you can build Guanxi with a sales person too. But not with factory workers because they might not care as much for your productions as someone who has a strong relationship with the factory owner.

Also, don't forget that any factory worker might find your product profitable and start copying you, and begin to sell those on eBay before your actual idea would even make it to US. However, when you have built a strong Guanxi with the factory owner, the factory workers would be scared of you, and would be more respectful.

So again, it's vital to be extra vigilant, and monitor Alibaba as well as eBay, even Amazon to be sure that your product or logo has not been copied without your knowledge. You should report anything you have found to the factory owner.

It's worth mentioning that Chinese people love to make money, and that's of course good news. The main focus in China is to make money in long term and in increasing amounts, so with the right understanding of the Chinese culture you should be just fine to do Business.

In order to illustrate my own personal experience, we will stick to e-mails only.

Thanks to the power of the internet, there is really no point in visiting China, at least not at first as we can visit all the factories virtually by heading over to Alibaba.com. Not only Alibaba, other huge websites also provide excellent opportunities for your supplier search, like Aliexpress, DHgate, or Global Sources.

I would highly recommend that you take a look at each website and begin to study them; how do they work, how to navigate on the site, understanding how to filter and so on. I would recommend another book that is dedicated to understand these websites: Passive Income – Platform Analysis by Sabi Shepherd. The book focuses on the above mentioned platforms and many others on how to leverage on each.

In case you just want to carry on and have a quick overview on the major differences of the main platforms where you can find Manufacturers, and suppliers for your product, I will explain what I personally recommend especially if you are a beginner.

When you visit a car sale boot, or a market, you see the people selling goods, and even the price listed, you can still negotiate, or just walk off.

When you visit web shops on the internet, there is a standard price for everything and with a click of a button you have placed your order and you will get your product 90% exactly the way it was pictured on the website, and in worse cases you can ask for a refund. It is a different case on Alibaba; you might look for a buy it now button but believe me there isn't' one there. You might think it's a mistake but what you find is an enquiry button instead.

If you are already thinking this is going to take some time, then you are absolutely right!

Alibaba vs Aliexpress

Aren't they the same? – Well they do sound similar and it's because both are owned by Alibaba Group.

Aliexpress has a built-in payment system and working in a way similar to Amazon or eBay. With a click on a button you place your order. However, you can contact some of the sellers and ask if they would do private label, but there are only a few.

In my experience they respond very slowly, and in most occasions I cannot find any website of the sellers, or any proof that they have an established Factory.

What I also found is that if you just want to buy a product, like 10 or 50, you can by clicking on buy it now, it's easy, no negotiation required, but not so much opportunity for private labelling, unless you want to resell unbranded products.

Alibaba has no built-in payment options. You must negotiate with the suppliers. However, everyone you find on the platform is willing to private-label for you, no question about that. If your inquiry is about 10 – 50 products, probably they don't even answer, because they want serious businesses to get in contact, and I will explain the approach shortly.

Both Alibaba and Aliexpress are inventions of Jack Ma, and I have watched at least 20-30 hours of interviews with him, that I would highly recommend to anyone, using YouTube.

This will give you more understanding, and comfort of using these platforms. Also, you will quickly realize that 80-90% of products that are made in China and being sold globally are indeed ideas that first took place as a negotiation process on Alibaba.com.

DHgate is very similar to Aliexpress, but I have never tried to look for any Private label supplier there. If you want to take a look feel free to do so, but I have only purchased unbranded products that I have re-sold after and to be honest the free shipping took ages.

Global Sources is something that you might consider. I personally did take a look, but not started negotiating with suppliers yet.

It has been known that Global Sources has better quality products, but also having higher prices and supplier choice compared to Alibaba.

In this book we are going to focus on Alibaba. My personal experience has thought me well on tricks and strategies for the best supplier selection and sourcing techniques, and you should get a huge value from it, and certainly would make you more comfortable to start your Business once you have grasped this knowledge.

How to avoid getting scammed

There are a couple of points here again that you should be aware of before we dive into Supplier selection. The most important is how not to get scammed.

I have already explained Guanxi and the importance of practicing it from the beginning. You must act like a pro, and also understand that some Chinese people are advertising themselves as excellent suppliers. You should also figure out how to eliminate scammers, and not even contact them by mistake.

There are just so many stories of people getting scammed on Alibaba, and I have read at least 50 of them all over the internet; on forums and different websites as well as on YouTube.

I have to say it's sad, and I really feel for people who have experienced getting scammed. However, in my view, most of these stories come to the point of not being prepared and acting like a newbie, not following the guidelines of Alibaba escrow system, going for cheap products, making payments on Western Union, and mainly not vetting the suppliers properly.

So, I hope you see that everything is about preparation and for that you must gain knowledge, and knowledge comes with information. Information must be learned in order to be successful, and even before being successful, not to get scammed.

When you see a sweet deal, but everyone else selling the same product for twice as much, well you should consider researching on that supplier a little bit deeper.

You can simply ask: Why is it so cheap? And once you get an answer you can go from there…

Payment methods:

You might find some suppliers don't list any payment methods. They might not be scammers, but you should raise the question as to why they are not listing any payment method? Just

Payment   This supplier also supports L/C,D/A,D/P,T/T,Western Union,MoneyGram,Paypal,Western union,Escrow service payments for offline orders

stay away from those kinds of suppliers.

Only option is Western Union: Stay away from them too.

You might find some of them only list escrow and bank transfers as payment method, and you will not see any PayPal

option like below:

TT – refers to an escrow system, very similar to PayPal that Alibaba built into the website, and it's very useful, as the money will not get released to the seller until you confirm that you have received what you ordered.

You have to also understand that PayPal is not very popular in China. This is due partly to the fact that when you make an order and pay via PayPal, the seller must pay 5% as PayPal fee from the Total Payment. Also, when you make a payment, the seller might only be able to withdraw that money after weeks.

When you negotiate with your suppliers for your first order some of them do allow you to use PayPal, however it's always you who must cover the 5% costs, as they will have to pay that to PayPal.

An example here: your first order is 100 Units of x, and it comes to $500 as the total payment via PayPal. Then you ask for an invoice, and once you get that you will see the payment of $500 for the products + $50 PayPal fee that equals to a total payment of $550.

This is how it goes and that's it. So, if you find someone who says otherwise, like there is no PayPal fee to pay, or it's more, or simply come up with some drama at the last minute that they have a problem with their PayPal, and you should wire money to the boss's account, that's a big NO-NO!

Stay away from scammers!

Another one is Western Union! Do not pay anyone through Western Union! Yes, they are nice. Yes, they have sent a free sample, bla bla…. Do not make Western Union payment to anyone under any circumstance. Well to be honest, I did hear stories like; at first payment it was PayPal, then wire transfer, and sometimes Western Union, and there was never any problem, and that's fine. But why take the risk especially when there are thousands of suppliers out there who are willing to take a PayPal at first then wire transfer which is way safer.

I do not intend to scare you away from Alibaba, but please be aware of the tricks that some might try to play on you. Always be extra vigilant. If there is a problem, just ask questions like, what is the problem? Does it happen often? Then once you get an answer, it should be common sense really. Do not get fooled by anyone.

Market language

There are few words that are very common to use when you place an order in China, and you should not give away yourself by not knowing their meaning, or even worse, not using them.

This will be the first impression when you introduce yourself, as there is a way to write and talk about things. Not like an average person, or newbie would, but like a pro who knows the deal.

Don't worry too much, only few acronyms you should remember, and you can always refer back to them from here:

- MOQ - Minimum order quantity

This just makes sense and should be easy to remember. It's vital to use MOQ, and avoid anything like, "How many can I order?" or even "Minimum order for items..."

- UNITS

Do not write, or mention the words "item", "items", "piece", "pieces". It's an easy give away that you are a newbie.

- QC- Quality Check

Instead of asking for "inspections" you might say or write QC instead.

- OEM – Original Equipment Manufacturer

This is how you ask for Branding a product. Do not mention words like: branding, private labelling, or white labelling, as Chinese suppliers might just get confused, so instead of explaining to them what private labelling means, you might just ask for "OEM 1000 Units".

- OEM Packaging

Custom packaging that should have your brand on it.

- ODM – Original Design Manufacturer

It really means the same as OEM; however, do not confuse your supplier, just stick with OEM. Please note: Many companies will list products with the availability of ODM, and that means OEM.

- FOB or AIR SHIPPING or AIR CARGO– *Free on board*

  This refers to a door to door delivery, normally using DHL, FEDEX, or UPS. This method is usually more expensive, but you can get the products within a week.

- SEA SHIPPING or CARGO SHIPPING

This is a method of shipping by sea, very cheap, however once you order this way, it will be your responsibility to get the containers to your home or to Amazon Warehouse.

- Freight forwarder

For this purpose, you can use many different companies, and their main responsibility is to pick up your containers from any port and deliver it to where you desire.

Additionally, many of these companies can also do Quality Checks for you. However, they are not cheap, but if you are not a US resident, that might be the only option if you are purchasing large quantities that might come in Shipping containers.

- SAMPLE ORDER

In case you something like a small order at first, and you really don't want to order more then 100 -300 Units, you might ask for a sample order.

If you mention "small order" to your supplier, they will know right then that you are a small Business, or an individual, and possibly just starting out. Meanwhile, when you mention "Sample order" to your suppliers, they will think that even as a sample you are not only ordering 1-2 units, but 100, meaning you must be a large company who can afford to order as large as 100 Units even as a sample order.

Now that you are able to speak the market language it's time to understand the differences between a Factory and a reseller.

Factory vs Reseller

Another tricky one here, but why should it really matter? First let's just mention that even experienced Amazon FBA sellers wouldn't be able tell even after sourcing for years from the same people, if their suppliers are resellers, or an actual factory.

Allow me to explain the main differences that you should be aware of when it comes to a supplier choice.

Factory

The main point is that you might see straight away that they only have typically one type of product, and in this example, I will use wood. When you visit their website, you might see listings such as wooden spoon, wooden chopping board, wooden bowl, wooden chopsticks, and so on.

Even if you want to sell stainless steel spoons as well, you will not see it on their listing. At this point you might be thinking of finding someone else who has wood and stainless steel too, but that would be a mistake.

When you contact them they may not be able to speak proper English, and might be struggling to explain your desire, due to the language barriers.

In regard to pricing you might see that they are very cheap, especially if you order a large quantity.

Reseller or trading companies

They have good English, and are willing to help with regards to anything, even if it is not listed on their website. You might see the listing and realize they are actually selling wooden chopping board, as well as stainless steel knifes, silicon spatulas, even waterproof speakers. When you look at the prices, it might seem to be more expensive. Another difference could be that their showroom might be in the city, somewhere nice, and will not be somewhere like a factory on the outskirt of the city.

A quick analysis as an overall understanding here is that you might think the resellers are better and indeed that's how it looks like. You think about your desire to sell different products in the same category, and not only wooden products, so you might go with the one who can supply stainless steel, as well as silicon, and you don't have to carry out another supplier research right? Well it sounds too good to be true, and this is the time when you should think again.

When you have a problem of any kind with the product, the factory will apologize and give you a discount for the next order. This is because they certainly want to continue working with you. On the other side, a reseller might move their office, and change their Company name, rather than go back to a factory and tell them off.

A trading company will stay with the factory and you might not get any compensation, even if you take pictures of the faulty products, and you can be nice as you want to be. A worse case might happen that one of the product lines completely goes wrong, and the reseller also acting as a middleman to someone else with the same product, might get another devastating complaint from the other Amazon seller. Instead of trying to find a solution the trading company will change their Company name right then, and by the time you realize the issues, you can't even contact anyone anymore, as they would disappear and likely rename their company.

Believe me there are plenty of stories like that, where people explain the situation like everything was going well for 500 units, then for 1000 Units. After going for 2000 units still no problem, they begin to trust the supplier and pay upfront for 10000 units, the lead manufacturing time being 4 weeks. When they run out of product on Amazon and want to find out the progress from the suppliers, suddenly they are unable to contact them anymore as they have completely disappeared from the whole Internet.

Not scaring away anyone, but you must be aware that if something happens, like an issue with a product, the reseller who supplies from multiple factories to hundreds of sellers, will usually rather stay with the factories.

Not every trading company will act like that. They might try to help as much as they can as far as it doesn't hurt them, especially money wise, and sure they have to fill a purpose too.

In China there are many factories with lots of goods ready to sell, however they don't speak good English, and are unaware of the usage of Alibaba. So, they need help from someone who understands the marketing world and is able to sell their products.

Another example is concerning the factory I use and I am always in contact with. Actually, the lady I am in contact with is the wife of the Factory owner, and she always tells me that they have to study English, as well as how to operate Alibaba website.

They have a small factory of 10-12 people working there. All of them are family members. They mainly produce TPU, PVC, silicon, nylon… No wood, no steal, nothing electric, or complicated, and that should be your aim too.

I really hope that all I have said about why you should be careful when choosing a supplier and the reasons why you should work with a factory make sense to you.

It's a huge benefit, and a wise choice, and for those reasons you should be able to identify the differences between a factory and a trading company at the beginning, instead of losing time and money.

So, we carry on with the assumption that you should go with a factory, but might still have difficulties to tell as the listing is only wooden products, but some of them are actually plastic.

It might happen that they are a factory but have friends who also have a smaller factory and listing those items too, so they could be an excellent choice, but you are just not sure and in doubt.

Before you reach out to them, on Alibaba usually list their address and telephone number as well as the Company name, with a quick Google map search you should be able to see that there is a factory, or at least their location.

I am now going to show you an example that with it you just cannot go wrong, and the facts behind it.

I am not into wood or anything wooden. However, I thought I might show an example that you can see right away who you are dealing with, a factory and not an actual trading company.

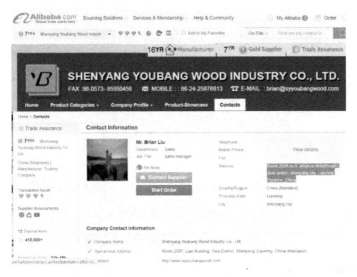

I am looking at only one thing that I can use to tell straight away that this factory will not rip you off, and that is the 7 years of being a Gold Supplier. Of course, I see they have fax number too, and trade insurance, but in order to be a gold supplier on Alibaba, you must pay Alibaba $3000 every year to get that.

So, in this case, they seemed to have been in the Business for 16 years, and they have been paying Alibaba every year for the last 7 years just to show that they provide quality.

I am personally not telling you to contact them, however, for me would be to see where their main market is. It's one good example that you might look at.

So back to this case, if I were to source product from China and resell them in the US, I personally wouldn't go with this Factory as it seems that their main market is Middle East, and Africa, even the third best is only North America, and those standards are just not the same as are in the US, or in Europe, but that's just me.

So now back in track trying to find out if a supplier who we really like is a factory or a reseller but having difficulties to know. What you want to do is just ask few questions to find out really.

Are you a factory or a trading company?

They may tell you straight away. In case the answer is not clear or they say they have a partner factory or anything that is unclear, then be sure they are a trading company and move on.

On the other hand, they will say what you want to hear. You should move on to your next question, something that is more technical, something that only the factory would know, and resellers wouldn't, something that is very specific in regards to the product, or the factory, and the machinery they use, or the quality check procedure.

Try even multiple questions, and if you get a reply like: Yes, we have quality control, but not very sure on the details, you will know who you are dealing with. However, on the other end you might get a very technical answer that would cover your entire questions and beyond.

Of course, the best is always to visit the factory, and truth be told I got multiple invitations from many factories, and once you begin contacting them, you will get them too.

Find the right Supplier

So many factors need to be taken into considerations, and it might be hard at first. If you have acknowledged beforehand and know that you are looking for a factory to be your supplier, you will know some facts already and understand that different products require different raw materials as well as different production lines. So, you should be filtering them out already. Using Alibaba gives you even more advantages for filtering options that you should use at all times when carrying out supplier research.

I know that I have explained few things already in regard to Alibaba. At first you shouldn't register yet. Simply look around having a good feel on how to navigate and understand the meaning of the free tools that you can use for your supplier research.

Once you register and visit Companies' websites, they will keep on contacting you with all sort of offers, and you will be flooded with e-mails too in your mailbox that you registered with. So, in case you already want to register, please use the name carefully as everyone on Alibaba will see you as that name and your e-mail address will be fully visible to all registered suppliers.

I will refer to the wood products again and say that you might use your own name. They might Google your name and even add you in LinkedIn, so it's up to you. But when getting registered, you may want to create a free Gmail account beforehand, like wood.sourcing@gmail.com or something like that, for their visibility it would make sense.

In the instance below, I simply searched for "wooden toys" and I already have 289,364 results. It's a little bit crazy; we really want to narrow down right at the beginning:

You should immediately start using the tools provided by Alibaba. Searching for nearly 300000 products would take forever.

At the top you already see that by default Alibaba search engine goes for products instead of Suppliers. So, once you choose that option you already have only 3914 suppliers:

That's still too much. Obviously want to get your best results, and for that, there are even more filters that you can apply:

Gold supplier – I already explained gold supplier and how to purchase it, and filtering that will narrow your search, but you should not stop there:

As you see the results are still 3901, so next filter to use is:

Trade assurance.

What Trade assurance provides is:

- Multiple safe payment options

- Worry-free shipping & Quality

- 100% on-time shipment protection

- Product quality protection

Using this filter already narrows it down to 2719 suppliers. That

of course is still too much:

There is still an option for filtering that you should always go for: Assessed Supplier.

The term Assessed Supplier simply means a supplier assessed by a third-party inspection company that Alibaba sent out to visit their actual location and make sure that everything is in place. To prove that, when you filter this, on each of those websites, there is an Assessment report available to view and download for your references.

That being ticked already filters out scammers and now you are only having 419 potential suppliers left to choose from. When you think about it, it does sound like a good choice, and

certainly better than 3900.

It's still very easy to get lost on who you should contact, and who actually replied. So what I suggest and personally did is to get your own excel spread sheet, and make a list of potential companies that you will get in contact with.

Please see below what I have created when I started out. I have removed everything that could lead you back to anyone, however hoping to help with the idea that you should follow in order to get organized.

Supplier research

I understand that might not be too visible, so I will list what I have done and helped me to filter even more when searching for suppliers.

- Date: It's the date I have sent the first e-mail to all 23 potential suppliers.
- Company name: You might easily see the difference, but to me it was like Shenzhen this, Shenzhen that... so I had no choice but to copy paste them.
- Companies Websites: Same as the Company name – it's better to have it rather than look for it again on Alibaba.
- Gold Suppliers: I wrote here the years – to be honest if someone has 1, or 2 years listed as a Gold supplier, they might not be your best choice. What I realized is that the English language barriers can cause difficulties when it comes to business. On the other hand, 6 – 8 years plus, I felt like they really want to push the MOQ

even for the first order to 5000 Units, and when I tried to negotiate with them, I didn't get any reply. So, your best bet in my opinion is to go with 3-5 years gold suppliers.

- Replied: Well they all replied within 48 hours anyways, at least for the first e-mail I sent out.
- Products: Here I have added few notes that I had in mind additionally for future ideas, and tried to avoid the ones who have only few listings.
- OEM: Who would private label for me?
- Contact Names: It's something that you are really going to need to refer back to, at least at the beginning, because when you send an e-mail on Alibaba, and you get a reply, you also get a reply to your Gmail and you might not see straight away what Company sent you that, only the person's name who actually sent it.
- Paypal: Just listed it in case of necessity. But these questions I only asked those 3 who I actually ordered sample units from.
- Sample Order: I eventually only ordered samples from 3 suppliers

- Ship to FBA: Those 3 I asked all said that's not a problem.

- Sample order paid: I have just added how much I already paid and so I also track who I made the payment to.

- Paypal account: Here I have added their PayPal address that they have provided for tracking purposes.

- Courier: I was tracking who is using what courier company and if there is any price differences, so I could choose the cheapest in future.

- Tracking Number: I have added here the courier tracking number that the suppliers provided me with.

You might create something better, something that is simpler. I am not a Microsoft Excel pro for sure; however this helped me so much at the beginning.

Once you get to the point of communicating only with one or two suppliers then you don't need this anymore. However, you can always refer back to it.

Alternatives to Alibaba

This chapter is dedicated to finding suppliers in an unusual way, beyond Alibaba. There are a few ways to find suppliers that I am going to elaborate on now:

1. Taobao

Taobao is the equivalent to EBay and Amazon based in China. It belongs to the Alibaba group. You will need to speak and read Chinese if you want to communicate with these suppliers.

Actually, most people on there are not suppliers but private persons, similar to EBay sellers.

If you are using Google Chrome you can auto-translate the site but be aware that the translation might not be accurate.

You can, however, find some great products and ideas if you auto-translate the site and its categories. You can browse through categories and if you see something that you like on there you could send it to your supplier and ask if he has any knowledge of this product and where to find it.

There are many items on there that you won't find on Aliexpress or Alibaba/Globalsources, mainly because these items are created for the Chinese market and taste.

BUT, you can find items or trends in China on there that could very well work in your country too. Remember, country specific trends could be your next great idea

2. Global sources magazine

I am really astonished on how little people know about this service. They usually update every category every few weeks/months. The content is amazing. High quality photos, descriptions, supplier details, trends, everything!

It's a great way of getting ideas and finding suppliers.

Have a look here and take a look at the many different product groups that they cover:

http://www.globalsources.com/gsol/GeneralManager?&catalog_id =2000000003844&design=clean&language=en&page=emag/Sou rcingMagazines&src=hdr&pi_proj=10AWJP&source=GSOLHP_ TopNav_MR

Another great service by Global Sources:

You can actually contact Global Sources and ask them anything for free (as long as you are registered). If you are looking for a product or a supplier of a specific product, maybe even in a specific area, they can help find it.

Check it out:

http://www.globalsources.com/SITE/BUYER-

SUPPORT.HTM?source=GSOLHP_TopNav_OS_BS

Insider's tip: Even if you can't go to an exhibition you can still find out about all the suppliers exhibiting there. How? Simply go onto the exhibition's website.

Then click on "Full Exhibitor List" and there you go. You have all exhibitors exhibiting at this fair. It's a bit of a lengthy process but you can check all websites of the suppliers, look at their products, and contact them directly without even going to the exhibition.

This applies to almost any exhibition in the world. By the way, this is also a great way to find potential CUSTOMERS. If you are planning to sell to retailers or wholesalers, you can also look at these exhibitor's lists and see them as a potential sales lead.

3. Baidu search

Baidu is the most used search engine in China (since Google is blocked). Everything is in Chinese, but just like Taobao you can auto-translate the page.

I use it sometimes to look for a specific product. It's like a supplier directory, listing a lot of suppliers. For example, if you type "handbag manufacturer" you will find mostly results that lead to Chinese companies. A few overseas websites are listed too but not as many as if you would use Google.

Baidu can also help you to find patents on items that you may be looking for.

Baidu has a separate website for that, called Baidu Zhuanli: http://zhuanli.baidu.cn/

Again, you can translate via auto-translate but it is very difficult to navigate if you don't read/speak Chinese. You can ask your supplier to check it for you.

How to find local fairs & wholesale markets

Prices are usually a little more expensive than from the factory since many of the companies there are trading companies or agents for factories.

Many cities in China have an "exhibition center" that houses all-year exhibitions or wholesale markets. Here is a list of some of the biggest wholesale markets/all year exhibitions in China:

The most famous one, housing everything from electronics to toothbrushes is in Yiwu.

YIWU MARKET

http://www.businessinsider.com/yiwu-china-largest-wholesale-market-2011-10?op=1#ixzz3V5meL6e8

http://en.wikipedia.org/wiki/Yiwu_market

Clothing wholesale markets

Guangzhou Baima market

www.baima.com

Address: 16 Zhannan Rd Guangzhou Guangdong Province

Humen Fumin Fashion City

www.fumin.com

Address: Humen Town, Dongguan City, Guangdong Province

Hangzhou Sijiqing apparel wholesale market

Over 1200 manufacturers with stores at this market. There is an annual sale of 6billion RMB reported from this market.

Address: 31-59 Hanghai Rd Hangzhou Zhejiang province

Furniture wholesale markets:

Shunde furniture wholesale market

The largest furniture wholesale market in China. It's actually 1 mall after another on that road. You could drive for 15 minutes along that road and you will still find showrooms of factories.

http://en.wikipedia.org/wiki/Shunde,_China_Furniture_Wholesale_Market

Electronics wholesale markets:

a. Shenzhen SEG Electronics Wholesale Market
    This market is China's largest electronics market and sits in between Shennan Road and North Huaqing road. It is located at the SEG plaza and occupies the first to the tenth floors. The market has over 3000 shops.

Address: Intersection of Mid Shennan Rd and North Huaqiang Rd, Shenzhen

http://en.wikipedia.org/wiki/SEG_Plaza

b. Shenzhen Huaqiang Electronics World (HEW)

This market is China's second largest electronics market and covers many categories.

There are 2800 stores that specialize in electronics and computers.

Address: No 1007—No 1015 North Huaqiang Rd, Shenzhen, Guangdong

c. Guangzhou Electronics Wholesale Market (GEC)

Guangzhou Electronics City (GEC) is a large-scale market that specializes in electrical equipment. It is located on the first floor of a newly built exhibition center that is to the west of the Guangzhou Cultural Park on Xidi Second Road. With more than 6000 m² business area and over 300 independent stores, it covers communication equipment, fax machines, telephones and various audio and photography equipment, as well as game consoles and other small electrical appliances.

Address: No 94 Liwan Rd, Guangzhou

Toys wholesale market:

a. Guangzhou International Toys & Gifts Centre

Located in the Guangzhou Huangpu International Logistics Park, the Guangzhou International Toys and Gifts Centre (GITGC), with 1.5 billion total investments, covers a total construction area of 320 thousand square meters, which makes it the largest toy and gift distribution center nationwide.

There are nearly 800 shops that are mainly in the form of street shops.

b. Beijing International Toys City (BITC)

Beijing International Toys City (BITC) has over 1000 shops. You will find famous domestic and international brands of toys of all kinds such as electronics, plush toys, woodwork, handicraft gifts, etc.

Address: No 67 South Third Ring Rd

c. China Toys & Amusement Facilities Wholesale Market

China Toys and Amusement Facilities Wholesale Market sits in Tianjia Wan of east Xianning Road in Xi'an. The market is divided into five areas, namely toys and children's articles, amusement facility wholesale, electric toys wholesale, fitness appliance wholesale and arts and crafts wholesale. There are approximately 300 stores.

Dealing with customs regulations

Whenever an importer calls me for a freight quote, my first question is "What are your sales terms with your supplier"? Invariably the importer replies that he's not sure. Sales Terms (officially known as Incoterms) tell WHO PAYS FOR WHAT AND FROM WHERE TO WHERE. They are extremely important in knowing what the true COST of your product is, before you place the order for your goods with the supplier. For instance, your supplier in China quotes a price to you for your "widgets" of US$1.00/widget and he then uses the term "FOB Port Shanghai". This means that the supplier is paying for all freight charges up to the Port of Shanghai (which includes the Chinese trucking charges and certain Handling and Customs fees in China) and your company will then pay for all charges from Port Shanghai to your final destination (which would include the ocean or air freight, USA customs entry fees, USA customs duties, any accessorial charges, and delivery to your final destination.

Listed below are the most frequently used Incoterms with a brief description for each:

EX-WORKS: The buyer (importer) bears all costs and risks involved for the shipment from the seller's premises to the final delivery destination. Also known as "ex-factory".

FOB (Free on Board): The buyer bears all costs and risks once the goods have crossed the rail of the ship at the port of export in the foreign country. The buyer should always insist on a "named place", i.e. FOB PORT SHANGHAI, to make the term crystal clear.

FAS (Free Alongside Ship): the buyer bears all costs and risks once the goods have been placed alongside the ship at the port of export in the foreign country. Again, always insist on a "named place". This term is not commonly used, except for some heavy machinery and equipment shipments, as it is confusing to even transportation professionals as to what charges are actually due from each party at the port of origin.

CFR (Costs and Freight): Also known as "C&F". The seller pays the costs and freight required in shipping the goods to a "named port of destination". The buyer's responsibility begins once the cargo has crossed the rail of the ship at the port of destination. An example would be "CFR Port Miami" for an import shipment to Port Miami.

CIF (Cost, Insurance and Freight): Same as CFR except seller also has to cover the cost of insuring the goods to the named place of destination.

DDP (Delivered, Duty Paid): The seller pays for all charges, including USA customs duty and USA delivery, to a named place.

DDU (Delivered, Duty Unpaid): The seller pays for all charges, excluding USA customs duty to a named place.

The most important point to remember about Incoterms is that YOU MUST INSIST ON A NAMED PLACE in the agreed upon terms. Too many times I see a supplier's commercial invoice with a very general Incoterms notation, leaving much in question if a disagreement were to take place over which party is to pay for which transportation charges. If your company was forced to sue a seller overseas because of a disagreement in charges, ANY court will first refer to the Incoterms notation on the seller's commercial invoice. Some case studies:

A German supplier quotes a price to you with Incoterms of "C&F USA". As you have determined from the previous descriptions, "C&F" means the supplier is paying for the "costs & freight" charge to the "USA", leaving you to pay for the USA Customs and final delivery charges. But the "USA" is a BIG PLACE, isn't it? In cases such as this, the importer assumes the supplier is quoting the charges to either the importer's door or to the nearest port or railhead (assuming it's an ocean shipment). I mean, after all, the importer knows that the supplier knows he's physically located in Wichita, KS, USA so certainly that's where he's being quoted to. RIGHT?! Well, in most cases, this supplier is simply quoting to the nearest USA port to HIM - NOT TO THE IMPORTER. Why? Because it's a lot cheaper to ship from Germany to Port New York than all the way to the Wichita railhead! And guess what? It will likely cost more to get this shipment from the East Coast port to Wichita than it cost the supplier to get it to the East Coast port. All of this means that your transportation costs just went up considerably! Another example: A supplier quotes a price "FOB Shanghai". Hmmmm… Does he mean from his factory in Shanghai or from the Port in Shanghai? If you are shipping an ocean container, that "unclear term" could mean a few hundred dollars to you, so you really need to narrow it down in order to negotiate your "per unit" costs knowledgably. And as you can see from the Incoterms above, there are better terms to use when from a factory dock door (such as Ex-Factory or Ex-Works). Therefore, ALWAYS name an exact place either at origin or destination for your sales contracts so there is no question from either party as to who is to pay for what transportation charges.

If you want to take responsibility for your supplier's factory door then you want "Ex-Works" terms. If you want your supplier to get the product to the nearest port of export in his country, then find out what it is and name it in your Purchase Order (i.e. Port Shanghai).

An IMPORTANT NOTE to think about when setting your SALES TERMS:

If your supplier is quoting ANY of the Incoterms where he is paying for all or part of the freight charges (C&F, CFR, DDP, DDU) he will likely insist on choosing the freight forwarder that will handle the cargo from point of origin to the named destination. This may be perfectly fine as the forwarder they choose may end up being a great service provider. HOWEVER, you HAVE now effectively given up control of what happens to your cargo when you allow someone else to choose the company that will be handling your precious goods. Understand this: YOU are paying for the transportation charges whether they actually come FREIGHT COLLECT or not. Products quoted "C&F" have higher Per Unit prices than those quoted "FOB" because the supplier has to cover the costs of getting the goods to whatever place he is quoting to. For instance, a "widget" might be quoted to you at US$1.00/widget on an EX-Works basis, and US$1.50/widget on an FOB Origin Port basis.

Just something for you to keep in mind since you are paying anyway.

Continuous Customs Bonds

Even though you will now also be checking on freight charges to get your products from there to here, I wanted to first introduce you to the need to go ahead and apply for a Continuous Customs Bond because it may take 2 to 6 weeks to become active. Continuous Bonds are valid for one year from date of issue and are required for all commercial import shipments to the USA (air or ocean). The Customs Bond basically assures U.S. Customs that it will receive any duties or fees due in the event your company is unable to pay after taking delivery of the goods (bankruptcy, etc). Until just a few years ago, companies that wanted to "dip their toe" into importing could purchase a "single entry Bond" for individual shipments. But security changes brought on by 9/11 have made it necessary to purchase a Continuous Bond now.

When applying for the Continuous Customs Bond you will be asked for a company financial statement and information about the products you intend to import, their Customs Classifications numbers and an estimate of duties you expect to pay over the next 12 months. The minimum Continuous Bond amount is

$50,000.00 and the vast majority of bonds are written for that amount.

DO NOT WAIT to apply for your Customs Bond, particularly if your company is new and has little or no financial history. These Bonds have become much harder to obtain, primarily because the cost for a year is only between $300 and $500. You can find Bond Underwriters through your Customs Broker or via a web search.

Choosing Freight Forwarders & Negotiating Freight Rates

FIRST THINGS FIRST: REGARDLESS OF THE SALES TERMS YOU AGREE TO WITH YOUR SUPPLIER, DO NOT ALLOW YOUR OVERSEAS SUPPLIER TO CONTROL THE CHOICE OF THE FREIGHT FORWARDER!!! Why? Because choosing your own freight forwarder allows you to control both your cost and the routing of your cargo to your final destination. It also has a benefit in that your freight forwarder is WORKING FOR YOU and will give you accurate and complete information about your shipment as events overseas transpire. If the supplier chooses the freight forwarder, that forwarder now works for the supplier (not you) and is then bound to do whatever the suppliers asks him to do, including possibly not being truthful about why a shipment is late. LISTEN TO ME: Many suppliers are not able to meet their production promises to their customers. Time and time again my import clients will alert me to contact a supplier to arrange a shipment and they've been told the shipment will be ready on a certain date, say September 15. I will then notify my agent in the city/country of the supplier to contact the supplier to arrange the shipment. Sure enough, the supplier will tell my agent the goods will be ready September 15. But, on September 13 or 14 the supplier will advise that the goods will now be ready on September 20. Since the importer is using the forwarder of THEIR choice, they are automatically notified of the new ready date and new booking details and new ETA to the USA. More often than now, had the supplier chose the freight forwarder, there would have been NO NOTIFICATION of a production delay and no mention of a later delivery date until the shipment was due to arrive in the USA. And when the importer questions the supplier about the delay, the supplier will typically blame it on the forwarder or the carrier since you don't have a relationship with the forwarder. Other problems that can arise when the supplier chooses:

Freight shows up in the USA unannounced, and sometimes in the wrong city. YES. THAT HAPPENS ALL THE TIME! The importer then has to scramble to get the supplier paid so the goods can be released and make arrangements to clear Customs and truck to the final destination. This may cost the importer hundreds of dollars more than planned.

The import documents aren't handled correctly by your supplier and/or freight forwarder and you have no way of knowing that until the freight has arrived. Note that, once a shipment arrives at the port or railhead or airport, the clock starts ticking on the amount of "free time" the carrier allows for you to clear Customs and take delivery. And storage charges are quite high, whether air or ocean freight. When you choose the forwarder, they will tell you prior to arrival if any documents are incorrect or additional documentation is necessary to make the Customs Entry.

No I.S.F. (Importer Security Filing) is filed by the supplier's freight forwarder and you are not provided with the shipment information prior to export so that you can arrange to have it filed. ISF is one of the security measures adopted after 9/11. All ocean shipments must have an ISF filed PRIOR to the shipment departing the foreign country. This allows U.S. Customs to stop a questionable shipment before it leaves the foreign port for the USA. There is currently a $10,000.00 fine per instance of failing to file ISF. So, if none of the other reasons for controlling the choice of forwarders appeals to you, THIS SHOULD!

Think of your freight forwarder as an extension of your own company who happens to be "on the ground" in the foreign country from which you are ordering your products.

There is an old adage in the freight forwarding business: THERE IS ALWAYS SOMEBODY CHEAPER. And it's true. There are literally tens of thousands of freight forwarders, large and small, worldwide. And every one of them wants your business, and every one of them will quote you the absolute lowest rate they can (even if they aren't making any money on your first few shipments) in order to obtain your business. It's that competitive for them!

Now I'll tell you another old adage from ANY industry: YOU GET WHAT YOU PAY FOR! And with you being a brand-new importer, the VERY LAST THING you should want to do is choose a forwarder based solely on the rate. My experience has been that an importer will switch forwarders for a savings of $50.00 out of a total freight invoice amount of $4000.00 and almost immediately be sorry they did either due to indifferent service or the rate really wasn't cheaper after all costs were considered. What I'm saying to you is this: Talk to several freight forwarders and ask to speak with their operations personnel that will handle the setup and tracking of your shipments and get a feel for them on the phone. Most forwarder sales people that come to your office can promise you anything, and many of them have no operational background. They are great for getting you rates, but they likely won't have any contact with the foreign agent entrusted to handle your shipment overseas or do any of the routing or paperwork to get it to the USA. If the rates are close to equal, choose the forwarder that provided you with the best information and that you felt was interested in your company and your needs.

The information the forwarder will need to know in order to provide you with quotes:

Exact origin per your Purchase Order Incoterms.

Destination in the USA where you want your cargo delivered.

Commodity (what you are shipping).

Gross weight and cubic meters (CBM) or cubic feet (CFT) -.

For air freight shipments they will also need the length, width & height of each piece of cargo due to size limitations in the belly of the aircraft.

Your transit time needs (fastest possible usually = most expensive).

To give you accurate quotes, the forwarders will likely have several other questions for you until they become more familiar with your account and what your (and your supplier's) particular needs are. Every shipment is different in some way and there are sometimes many ways to route a shipment from Point A to Point B, resulting in different transit times and rates. Some case studies:

You have a client in Birmingham, AL for whom you'll be shipping ocean containers of your product from China. There are several ways to get ocean containers from China to Birmingham:

A. Via an ALLWATER Service through the Panama Canal to Port Savannah and truck to final destination in Birmingham. To a novice, this service would seem to be the wrong way to ship because you are bypassing the Gulf Coast for the East Coast, however, there are many different vessels sailing every week to the East Coast and most of those vessels offer a China Port to Savannah Port transit time of about 30 days. Additionally, since so many vessels are calling Savannah, rates are very competitive - even when you add in the trucking cost to Birmingham.

B. Via an ALLWATER Service through the Panama Canal to Port Mobile and truck to Birmingham. Ah, you say, that's the correct routing. Well maybe NOT - Mobile has very few vessels weekly from China so the ocean rates are usually higher than to Savannah. Additionally, the transit time to Mobile will usually be about a week longer than to Savannah. And if you check an atlas, Birmingham is 385 miles from Savannah and 260 miles from Mobile - a difference of about $250.00 in trucking charges. That trucking difference could be made up by the savings in the ocean freight to Savannah versus Moblie.

C. MINILANDBRIDGE Service via the West Coast with rail to Birmingham. MLB service is almost always the fastest transit time, and usually the most expensive as well. And you will still have to deliver the cargo by a truck once the container arrives at the railroad in Birmingham. In this instance, your MLB transit time will likely drop down to between 23 and 26 days (versus the 30 day transit to Savannah and the 37-40 day transit to Mobile). Your cost via this option may be more than via Savannah, but there are too many variables for me to give you a hard and fast rule in this particular instance. This is why it's important for you to have your forwarder check your options.

Another scenario: You have an air freight shipment going from Germany to Phoenix, AZ. Your likely routing options are:

A. Direct flight to Los Angeles Airport (LAX), clear Customs there and then truck to your client in Phoenix. While you would normally want to route any air shipment to the nearest airport city to your final client, this IS a valid option as there are several flights daily from German airports to LAX. And there are several truckers that run LAX to Phoenix nightly as well.

B. Route with the airline all the way to Phoenix Airport (PHX), clear Customs at PHX and truck to your client locally. This is also a valid option, but you should note that it is very likely the airline will fly your shipment to LAX anyway and then truck it themselves to PHX. So, this option may take a couple of days longer to actually deliver to your client, and it may even be a little more expensive than "A" as well.

One final scenario: You have an ocean shipment that is too small to ship in a container by itself and you don't want to pay the much higher air freight charges. Your only option is to ship LCL (Less Than Containerload) ocean freight. Your shipper is in India and your client is in Cleveland, OH. As with air freight, you typically want to route your shipment to the nearest Customs clearance point to your final delivery address. Cleveland IS a Customs Airport city, so you should ask your forwarders for rates to both Cleveland as a "direct shipment", and to an East Coast or West Coast port with Customs clearance at that port and then truck to your Cleveland client from that port. In these cases, you really never know which will end up being the least expensive or the fastest transit. So, it's important to check all options.

BOTTOM LINE: Regardless of your origin or final destination or mode of shipping, ask your freight forwarders for quotes based on various rates and service levels so you can decide the best fit for your particular shipments. Your needs will change from shipment to shipment as your client may need some product faster one month than the previous months. By knowing your various options, you can shave freight cost and/or transit time depending on your needs for that particular shipment. THERE IS RARELY ONLY ONE WAY TO ROUTE A SHIPMENT, SO ASK FOR YOUR OPTIONS AND YOUR FORWARDER'S RECOMMENDATION BASED ON YOUR NEEDS FOR THAT PARTICULAR SHIPMENT.

Choosing A Customs Broker

OK, you've now chosen the freight forwarder for your initial shipments. What about the Customs Clearance once the shipments arrive in the USA?

Customs Brokers file the Customs Entry with U.S. Customs upon importation of your products. They receive an Arrival Notice from the Freight Forwarder (either directly or from you) and the commercial invoice/packing list/related documents from you and submit the entry for Customs perusal and release. Customs Brokers also deal directly with Customs and other governmental agencies such as the FDA, FCC, and USDA if applicable for your products. If your shipment is held up for a physical Customs inspection or exam, your Customs Broker will make all arrangements and notify you if additional information is being required by the agency. And, if you import into different parts of the USA, you no longer have to use different Customs Brokers in different cities - you can use your chosen Broker in virtually any port/airport/border crossing now due to Remote Location Filing (RLF). I will caution you that, when you are interviewing prospective Customs Brokers, be sure and ask them if they have RLF abilities.

Most of my clients over the years have preferred to have "One Point of Contact" for their international shipping - meaning they use a Freight Forwarder that is also a Customs Broker or vice versa. Or sometimes they use a Freight Forwarder who then appoints the Customs Broker, and that Forwarder then does all interface with the Broker for your account - so you're only dealing with one party. I would highly recommend this "One Point of Contact" service as you never have to wonder who to call when you have a question. Most new importers wouldn't know when the Forwarders responsibility for a shipment ends and when the Brokers began, so just make it easy on yourself and choose a One Point of Contact service.

As with Freight Forwarder selection, choose the Customs Broker that you feel most comfortable with and you feel can handle your shipment in any Customs clearance point in the USA. Customs Brokers fees are typically very reasonable (average of $100 per entry nationally) and don't vary very much from broker to broker.

Inland Freight

Since you need to know your total product costs to your warehouse or your customer's destination BEFORE you quote a final price to your client, you should have the Freight Forwarder quote the inland freight at the same time he quotes you the international shipping. That is MY recommendation. But you have 3 options for handling the inland freight to your warehouse or client's place of delivery:

A. Ask the freight forwarder when obtaining the international freight quote (as described above).

B. Ask the Customs Broker to quote it, but since the shipment won't be in the USA when you're getting this quote, you will need to provide them with the exact shipment details.

C. Handle it yourself through your own trucking contacts.

Because there are so many arrangements to make to get an international shipment sourced and moved to the USA, you may consider the Inland Freight cost and service to be an afterthought. DON'T!!! Due partially to the high costs of fuel, Inland Freight charges in some instances are even higher than the international freight charges themselves. Inland Freight service and charges are the main reason why I advocate routing an air or ocean shipment to the nearest port or airport city to your final destination.

Here are a few case studies of actual shipments I've handled showing Inland Freight charges when compared to the ocean and air freight charges themselves:

A. An LCL ocean shipment from Port Ningbo, China with a final destination of Scranton, PA. The shipment was very small: 0.59 cubic meters & 129 pounds gross weight. The shipment was routed to Port New York where it was cleared through Customs and was delivered by truck to Scranton. Charges were:

LCL Ocean Freight= $125.00 (this was the Minimum Charge for this LCL shipment)

N.Y. Warehousing= $318.50 (YES, New York warehousing charges are expensive!)

Inland Freight to Scranton = $109.00

So as you can see, in this case, the Inland Freight from New York to Scranton (a distance of 100 miles) is very close to the Ocean Freight from Ningbo to New York (7500 miles). And each PALED in comparison to those New York warehousing charges (which are charged for trucking the container to a warehouse and unloading it into the individual LCL Ocean shipments).

B. An Air Freight Shipment from Shanghai Airport with a final destination of Bismarck, ND. The shipment had a gross weight of 160 pounds and a "chargeable weight" of 220 pounds. The shipment was routed to the nearest Customs Airport (Minneapolis), where it cleared Customs and was then truck delivered to Bismarck. Charges were:

Air Freight= $595.00

Inland Freight to Bismarck = $137.87

C. A full container ocean shipment (40 foot) from Port Xiamen, China to a final destination of Tucson, AZ. The container was routed to Port Los Angeles where it cleared Customs and was then trucked to the client's facility in Tucson by the steamship line's trucker. Since this is a full container ocean shipment, the Inland Freight portion of the rate is figured on the mileage from L.A. to Tucson, instead of the weight of the shipment itself. Charges were:

40Ft Container Ocean Freight to Port L.A. = $2700.00

Inland Freight from L.A. to Tucson= $2000.00

The above examples give you an idea of how important the Inland Freight charges can be when you are figuring your total product costs (i.e. landed costs).

Accessorial (Other) Transportation Charges

Where to start? There are many and varied "accessorial" transportation charges, some are fairly standard and can be planned for, while others are "one time" charges due to a Customs examination or storage fees due to a delay in the release of your cargo. I attempt below to outline normal, everyday accessorial fees by Mode of Transport, but please note that this is not a complete list due to variances at each port of entry and of products themselves. Also note that all of these accessorial Fees will be paid by your Customs Broker or Freight Forwarder on your behalf (with your written permission) and included in your invoice from them.

AIR FREIGHT SHIPMENT ACCESSORIAL FEES

AIRLINE FEES: These vary by airline and by port of entry but will normally be in the $40.00 to $50.00 range per airbill of lading.

PALLET CHARGES: Since most air freight is taken off of any pallets at the origin airport, most airlines require you to now pay a $5.00 to $10.00 per pallet fee to move your goods from their warehouse dock to your chosen trucker. Or you can ask your trucker to take empty pallets to "swap" with the airline, but your trucker will then charge you for pallets anyway.

STORAGE CHARGES: The airlines typically only give you 2 days to get a shipment cleared through Customs and off their dock. Should you be late for any reason, the Storage Charge at most airports will be approximately $40.00 Minimum or $0.05/pound (whichever is greater).

FULL CONTAINER OCEAN FREIGHT ACCESSORIAL FEES

CHASSIS RENTAL CHARGES: This is a new fee. Until 2012, the steamship lines in the USA owned or leased their own chassis (which are the wheels the container is mounted on for the road transport). But chassis require maintenance for tires and brakes and it was a money losing proposition for the carriers since they allowed chassis usage for free. Consequently, importers and exporters now have to pay for the use of the chassis while the container is being delivered. This charge varies from port to port and railhead to railhead but usually is $20.00 to $30.00 per day and you can typically count on the chassis being out for 2 days.

CUSTOMS X-RAY EXAM (sometimes termed VACIS Exam): More and more ocean containers are being x-rayed for security purposes upon arrival. And we've been advised that, in the near future, ALL import containers will be x-rayed. This is another security measure brought on by 9/11. This charge will vary by port or railhead as well but is usually between $250.00 & $300.00 per container.

STORAGE or DEMURRAGE: Ocean containers that are Customs cleared in ports are given either 4 or 5 working days of free time before storage starts. That's how long you have to clear Customs and remove the container from the port's yard. Working Days are Monday-Friday. Storage on port containers are usually charged at the rate of between $80.00 and $225.00 per day, depending on the port or the steamship line. Ocean containers that are Customs cleared at a railhead receive either 1, 2, or 3 working days free time, again depending on the railhead or the steamship line. Rail demurrage runs between $60.00 and $200.00 per day.

PIERPASS FEES (Ports L.A./Long Beach only): containers entering Port L.A. or Port Long Beach and clearing Customs there must pay a Pierpass fee of $60.00/20ft or $120.00/40ft container.

LCL OCEAN ACCESSORIALS
DESTINATION WAREHOUSING CHARGES: since LCL ocean shipments are commingled with many other LCL shipments in one container at origin, a Customs Bonded Warehouse at destination must pick the container up at the port or railhead and unload it back into the individual LCL shipments for Customs clearance purposes. Unfortunately, these charges vary wildly by destination, primarily depending on the costs to do business in the destination city. I have seen many instances over the years where the Destination Warehousing Charges were higher than either the ocean freight or the inland freight. Therefore it's very important that you make certain your Forwarder or Customs Broker quotes these charges when you obtain your freight quote.

CUSTOMS BROKERS CHARGES
CUSTOMS ENTRY FEE: While this is NOT an Accessorial Fee, this is the fee the Customs Broker charges to make the

Customs Entry on your behalf. ANY OTHER FEE that the Broker wants to charge you should be considered an Accessorial Fee. Most Customs Brokers charge an Entry Fee of between $75.00 and $150.00 per entry. The Entry Fee should be based on the complexity of your entries (i.e. what types of products you import and what governmental agencies have to be involved in the release). So you should talk with your Broker about what is required for your particular entries and then negotiate your Entry Fee accordingly.

FDA or FCC ENTRY: Brokers will (and should) charge you a small fee to submit documents to these agencies if required for your products. Typically, you should not pay more than $25.00 for this service unless the agency requires the Broker to also courier your documents to them.

COURIER FEE: Should the Broker be required to courier any documents or checks overnight on your behalf, they should be reimbursed for that expense with a slight handling fee on top of the cost. Courier Fees should not exceed $25.00 in most instances.

ADDITIONAL CLASSIFICATION FEES: Many brokers will try and charge a fee for each additional Customs classification on the Entry itself. If you are importing machinery parts and have 15, 20, 30 different classifications then you should expect to pay for the time it takes the Broker to go through your invoice and classify each individual product. This fee is negotiable however and you should talk with your Broker when you first get quotes from them, so you will know if your Customs Entries are more complex than the norm. My thoughts: sit down with your Customs Broker when you first start importing and give them a full list of the products with accurate descriptions. Offer to pay the Broker to classify the products up front and waive the "Additional Classification Fee" on entries thereafter, and then make certain that your supplier uses the exact same descriptions on his invoice every time you have a shipment. However, if you continually order "new products," then you should really expect to pay for the classifications as they arise. The biggest problem Brokers have in trying to classify merchandise is that the supplier's don't always use the correct description due to English not being their first language. An Example: an importer recently brought in a variety of furniture and home accessories - about 100 different items on the invoice. One item listed had a description of "bedding". When we checked with the importer, we found that the "bedding" was actually "sleeping bags". Another line item was for "copper lamp". We checked with the importer and it was actually an "iron lamp painted copper". When you think about it, those descriptions are pretty darned accurate for a foreign supplier - HOWEVER, FOR CUSTOMS, the actual description totally changed the classification and duty rate. It is the Importer's responsibility to tell his supplier the description of each item you are ordering. You cannot assume that anyone other than you and the supplier know exactly what you are shipping. Misclassification of products when making entry to U.S. Customs can result in fines and penalties and it is the Importer's responsibility to be sure they are correctly entered. IMPORTER SECURITY FILING FEE (ISF): Before getting into this fee, I want to discuss this requirement in more detail. An ISF is required for all ocean freight shipments destined for the USA. It is another result of 9/11. Essentially, U.S. Customs is given all pertinent shipment information (supplier name and address, where the container is being loaded, overseas forwarder name and address, commodities being shipped, vessel name, sailing date, USA arrival date, importer name and address, and final destination company name and address) by computer PRIOR to the shipment being loaded on the vessel in the foreign country. This pre-notification allows U.S. Customs to stop a shipment from being loaded on a vessel if they feel it represents a security threat and needs to be inspected. As the importer, it is YOUR responsibility to make sure the ISF is filed. Failure to file ISF in a timely manner can result in a penalty of up to $10,000.00 to the importer. This is YET ANOTHER REASON FOR YOU TO CHOOSE THE FREIGHT FORWARDER FOR YOUR SHIPMENTS! Time and time again I see importers allowing their supplier to make the forwarder choice and then the shipment arrives in the USA and we file the Customs Entry and find out no ISF was ever filed on the shipment. You have to understand that foreign suppliers DO NOT KNOW the regulations of U.S. Customs. My recommendation to you is to have your Freight Forwarder arrange to file the ISF for your shipments. Regardless of who files your ISF, expect to pay approximately $25.00 to $50.00 per filing.

DELIVERY ORDER FEE: unless you are having your Broker arrange the Inland Freight for your shipment, they will likely charge you a Delivery Order Fee for the preparation of the Truck Bill of Lading that is needed for your trucker to pick up the cargo at the port or railhead. This is a valid fee but you should try and negotiate it down to no more than $10.00 or so.

ADVANCED FUNDS FEE: the second most important function your Broker will provide you is when they advance small charges such as Airline Fees, Destination Warehousing Charges, and Customs Exam fees on your behalf. Since this saves you the hassle, and courier fees, of cutting all those small checks yourself, it is a valid fee and should be based on a percentage of the amount that was advanced with a low minimum fee. Some Brokers don't bother to charge this fee on small items. PLEASE DON'T expect your Broker to advance large sums of money for ocean freight and the like on your behalf - no one loans money for free for long!

Which method is best for you?

Online Product Sourcing Directories

Most people are somewhat familiar with "Alibaba" or have at least heard the name being thrown around here and there. Alibaba is essentially the 'holy-grail' when it comes to sourcing products from China. If you're not familiar with Alibaba, think of it as eBay on steroids. Instead of buying a single item, you find manufacturers for the products listed on Alibaba, which you can then contact to make bulk orders from. (By bulk we're talking orders of one hundred to tens of thousands of units. Yes… eBay on steroids.)

In short, this is how sourcing directories work, manufacturers sign up to the directory and put up product listings (much like eBay), and they then list the relevant details for the product and the factory, including the factory production capability, company bio, minimum order quantities, price range for the product, what materials are used to make the product and so forth. Ultimately, product sourcing directories are like shopping malls where you can go to get in touch with suppliers. Alibaba is the biggest online sourcing directory there is however it's not the only one; we will discuss some of our favorite alternatives later in this chapter. We will also briefly touch on how to best navigate and browse Alibaba in Chapter 6.

For now we will focus on the alternatives and what the pros and cons are of each. It's quite easy to navigate sourcing directories and they are quite similar in nature so you will be able to pick up how to use them quickly over time. For now, we'll go through the pros and cons of using Alibaba. (Also, if you've never visited Alibaba go check it out now if possible, the link is www.alibaba.com).

PROS

- Largest marketplace for finding suppliers in China and has the largest variety of products. (If you're having trouble finding a product on Alibaba, you're best alternative is to go to a product fair in person or ask a manufacturer to custom design what it is you're looking for.)
- Greater variety and more suppliers provide buyers – that's us! - more quotes and options. The more options we have, the more 'power' we have as we have the flexibility to walk away from certain suppliers or use competing quotes to negotiate for lower prices.

- Alibaba and any other sourcing directory is the fastest and easiest way to source products online - and all from the comfort of your home!
- Small minimum order quantities (MOQ) are accepted (~50 to 500 units is generally considered small depending on the price of the product)
- Potential risks and issues are minor and can be resolved easily with suppliers as long as due diligence is done to find reputable suppliers.
- Manufacturers on Alibaba are willing to work with smaller businesses and smaller minimum order quantities. (If you try placing orders with manufacturers in Western Countries at best you will get a polite decline, at worst you'll get laughed at. It's possible to work with some Western manufacturers and we'll get more into that later.)

CONS

- As it is the largest marketplace, scammers target people here. Luckily, scammers are easily discovered and avoidable.

- Many trading agents and trading companies pretend to be manufacturers on Alibaba and charge a premium for the products they sell to earn their profit.

- The number of product listings and manufacturers can be overwhelming. Especially when suppliers list the same products ten times with slightly different product photos. You will notice the same products being listed by multiple suppliers. These are generally trading companies listing the same product from the one manufacturer they all source from. (Filters help to easily cull the number of suppliers and minimize the total number of potential suppliers)

- Most factories quote a 'Western' price to foreigners which are higher than the prices they quote locally. In the end, 'foreigner' prices are still much better than what we can get in our own backyards. [Tip: if you can speak and write Mandarin or know someone that can, you can use this to your advantage by contacting suppliers over the phone or email to ask for quotes as they may assume you're a local and provide you 'local' quotes]

There are many, many product sourcing directories, and Alibaba isn't the only one available. Thankfully there are only three other sourcing directories that we recommend. These directories are smaller in terms of the number of suppliers and in the variety of products available when compared to Alibaba.

Product Sourcing Directory Alternatives

The product sourcing alternatives are listed below in order of preference:

1. www.HKTDC.com (Hong Kong Trade Development Council)
2. www.Made-in-China.com (ENSURE you go to Made-In-China with dashes, and NOT madeinchina as they are different websites)
3. www.GlobalSources.com

HKTDC and Made-in-China (MIC) are the preferred go-to websites as they have higher quality verification undertaken for their verified suppliers. As a result of more stringent measures, there are a smaller number of manufacturers and thus products, to search for. If you're able to find a manufacturer that is verified through either of these platforms, you can be certain you're dealing with a reputable supplier. We at the Mastermind differ in our personal preferences for sourcing directories; some browse

HKTDC and MIC first before we try Alibaba or Global Sources as reputable suppliers can be found more easily on the former; however, the overall time taken to source products is much less when using only Alibaba or Global Sources.

HKTDC

Verified suppliers on HKTDC have had their backgrounds and companies checked out thoroughly. As a result, suppliers that are verified on HKTDC are generally more reputable and of a 'higher quality' than suppliers found from other sourcing directories as they have been audited and inspected thoroughly.

Compliance verified suppliers on HKTDC have had the factory's manufacturing capability and social compliance standards (fair employee practices and environmental compliance) checked and audited. Several other audits and background checks are performed on HKTDC such as DUNS number (Dun & Bradstreet verified) and Intertek verified (certification for Corporate Social Responsibility). HKTDC also provides certainty about supplier certificates displayed on their website which is an added bonus that will save you time. If any certificates have "Intertek Verified" or have "Certificates Verified" then you can be certain that they are legitimate.

Other than providing verification as to the type of supplier they are (manufacturer, trader or wholesaler) there are other benefits to dealing with verified suppliers. As they have been verified, they do not want to lose good standing on HKTDC by receiving any negative reviews or complaints from buyers after going through such stringent audits, so they are more apt to treat buyers well. As suppliers have opted for these inspections to be undertaken, it also demonstrates they're not afraid to show what they are capable of and to unveil what lies under the drapes so to speak.

There's a free HKTDC trade magazine on their website which you can browse to source suppliers and product ideas from. When you sign up as a free member to these sourcing websites, we recommend you sign up with a spare email account as they send out frequent emails. Most of which are generally useless. It's also possible for suppliers to access your contact details and send you unwarranted offers so using a spare email will reduce any undesirable emails. Otherwise make sure to unsubscribe from unrelated notification emails in your account settings and increase your privacy settings so that your details are not shared openly with others that frequent the site.

A cheeky method to get good deals on HKTDC is to look for suppliers that aren't listed as "Accept Small Order". It's possible to score better prices in the beginning with such suppliers by negotiating your first order down to a lower minimum order quantity then they have listed. As these suppliers do not advertise for small orders, their prices and quotes have been set at a rate applicable to larger quantity orders and hence are cheaper. However, if you are able to negotiate for the same (or close to the same) prices at a lower MOQ then is listed, you have scored yourself a good deal. If you can't find the product you're looking for on HKTDC then move on and try Made-in-China.

Made-in-China

Made-in-China (MIC) also has a thorough audit system in place; as a result, their verified suppliers can be trusted. MIC provides free audit reports to download on suppliers that have been audited (look for the "Audited Suppliers" tag or filter). These reports provide extensive details on manufacturers and it's highly recommended that you read through them for any suppliers you order from. To access the reports, you will need to sign up as a free member. These reports are generally performed by SGS or Bureau Veritas, both highly reputable inspection companies. For best results, we recommend working with audited suppliers on MIC or HKTDC when possible. (It is worth repeating! **Please do not mistake Made-in-China with madeinchina.com as they are separate websites.** Avoid madeinchina.com when it comes to sourcing for suppliers.)

Global Sources

Global Sources (GS) is much like Alibaba, the only real differences are that it is lesser known to Westerners and has a smaller marketplace. We have found suppliers on GS to be better in terms of communication and English for some reason (maybe you can confirm if this is the case for you too!) There is a ton of free information on the GS website. You can check out their e-Magazines, tradeshows, catalogs etc. You will need to register for free to gain access to most of this information.

Verified checks for suppliers on GS are arguably better than Alibaba, however the audit and verification processes on GS and Alibaba are still 'primitive' considering the risk that buyer's face and the amount of capital at stake. On Global Sources you are less likely to be sourcing from the same manufacturer that your direct competitors use as it is not commonly used by most private labelers with Alibaba instead being their number one choice.

The Darkside of Alibaba and Global Sources

So why is it that some of us prefer sourcing from HKTDC and MIC over AB and GS?

As the number of suppliers is much smaller on HKTDC and MIC you won't always be able to source products here but we believe it is worth checking these websites first before heading on over to AB and GS... Otherwise known as the dark side to some us for these following reasons...

The verification process for Alibaba is deadly simple. It involves checking with relevant Chinese authorities that a supplier's name and address have been registered and not much else is done beyond that.

Gold supplier statuses on Alibaba are simply annual fees that suppliers pay Alibaba so that they are 'awarded' the Gold supplier badge. Currently there are three different payment packages: basic, standard, and premium. They range from $1,399 to a $6499 annual fee to receive the gold supplier badge. Check it out for yourself here: http://oak.alibaba.com/apply/upgrade_to_goldsupplier.htm; You will need an Alibaba account to view the rates. It is possible for suppliers to pay extra on top of these fees to have more serious verification undertaken. However, if most buyers only care about the Gold supplier status there is no real incentive for them to have further verification done at their own cost and time. Unless of course they are legitimate manufacturers with good standing and are confident that further verification will improve their chances in wooing buyers. Also note traders and wholesalers would clearly not undertake these additional audits or checks as they have no factories to get audited!

A lot of the suppliers on these directories not only lie about being manufacturers but they also 'lie' about factory details and products. Most don't do this intentionally as it is more of a case of them simply copying and pasting competitor product listing details into their own listings without checking them to ensure the details apply to them. This happens for a myriad of reasons including laziness and lack of confidence in their English writing abilities. You may find that factories claim to have certain factory standards, certifications or regulations on their product listing page but when queried through email they will state they do not have them.

Some suppliers also tend to use photos of products they find on Google or Amazon rather than taking pictures of their own, so do note there may be slight differences of what you see on the product listing and the samples you receive. It's best to get them to send you a photo of the product in the factory or at a tradeshow if possible.

Alibaba Trade Assurance and GS Verified Suppliers

Alibaba's Trade Assurance is not as safe as they make it out to be. If you spend some time reading through their complex terms and conditions you will see that it is not that secure of a payment solution. Most notably, in their T&Cs it states Alibaba have the absolute right to decide if your money is handed over to the supplier **AND** that there is no right of appeal to this decision.

Somewhere else in the terms and conditions it also states that claims that a product is faulty **must be made before goods are delivered** (this is only possible by performing or having an inspection done at the factory before shipment is made!) These are the two most glaring issues with Alibaba's trade assurance however there are many others spread throughout their terms and conditions.

Global Sources has a similarly weak verification procedure for their suppliers and automatically awards 3 stars to new suppliers (out of a 6 star rating system). Only this time, it costs $5480 to become a verified supplier on Global Sources so at least you know if they are verified they are unlikely to be scammers and have the budget and money to spend on marketing and advertising.

Conclusion

That wraps it up for book!

Thank you for purchasing this book and we hope it will aid you with your private label empire!

Your next steps from here will be making an order, booking an inspection for your order, and setting up your Amazon Seller Central account, product listings, packaging and photos.